Escaping the Housework

Book Three

Sylvia Charlewood

SpringwoodHouse Publishing

Copyright Sylvia Charlewood 2015

Escaping the Housework

First Published in the UK by SpringwoodHouse Publishing

12, Hillands Drive, Gloucestershire,GL53 9EU.

Other Titles in this Series:
Escaping the Housework 1 - Sylvia Charlewood
Escaping the Housework 2 - Sylvia Charlewood

ISBN978-0-9929255-5-0

Foreword

A further selection of musings from between the laundry and washing up!
Thanks again to the unfailing patience of my son, who has type-set and
done all the work,giving me the oportunity to offer some praise to my
favourite poet. I write of my own life and the world as I see it it in my home
and garden.

Table of Contents

1 - Le Pic Du Midi.

The mountain is terrible,
beautiful, too.
From the top,
the stars hang
like droplets
you can gather –
run through your hands,
like diamond water.
The summit is ice:
cold,blue; grey
with old snow;
another world,
far, far away
from green lands
down below.
Warm green lands -
where peaches grow,
wine is made,
people laugh,
are friendly.
And all the time
the mountains,
like rock crystal
piled up high,
watch over all,
and the winds
in the pines sigh.

September 2014-09-19

2 - Refugee

The moon still shines,
Cold comfort, on my bed;
upon my pillow
Famine lays her head.

Want took my youth,
and Grief will have my prime,
Disease will take my old age,
in good time.

Death takes my children,
one by one his kin.
Wind covets my poor rages,
to wrap him in.

My home is Nowhere,
and my country Woe.
nameless and starven,
through your lives I go.

Oxfam Poster, seen 1970

3 -   **Bagnères de Bigorre, Below the Pic Du Midi.**

This is somewhere
that, with shutters open,
you could grasp the moon,
or steal the stars,
night is so clear.
Water bubbles,
hot, from the earth here,
and people sing.
Buildings of all eras dream,
comfortably together,
standing around the Place,
and up and down
the little streets,
to oversee the market:
the happy stream
of shoppers,
cake nibblers,
peach sellers,
buyers of treats,
knots of chatterers –
beautiful, bustling,
friendly town,
below the Pic du Midi!.
2013

4 - Vaughan Williams on the Theme of Thomas Tallis.

Music such as this
so English, blithe,
and beautiful it is,
singing of Cotswold
trees and streams,
light moving over Severn,
running to the sea.
High hills and starry sky,
and fields that fold
around them, ploughed
or pasture land. And inns
where lights stream our
across the dark, and
men can drink and sing
as English boys and men
forever have sung, at the plough
or in the Parish Church:
times change:some keep the skill,
maintain old fashions fresh,
and old songs singing still.
See how the moon on Crickley
rises now. Traffic will come
and go: Crickley rises still,
and Daglingworth and Itlay
nestle, cosy, under hill.
All this the music speaks
for he who wrote lived near -
Down Ampney is not far!
So in respect, just drop a tear
for Tallis and Vaughan Williams
 who with well tuned English arts
wrote such glorious music
from their loving English hearts! March 2015

5 - And you still sing.

And you still sing, Beloved,
the same song that ever you have sung
of Truth and Reason, Liberty; still young,
your voice is echoing, along the years,
the aria of Freedom, mixed with woe;
of loveliness en-wrought with tears -
and still along that selfsame path you go.

And you still bleed, Beloved,
from that same hurt that wounded you,
not knowing if your heart would find one true,
kindred and closer, to that open heart –
you could not silence all its glowing art,
but always cried aloud for Liberty.

And you still ache, Beloved,
from that same pain you ever felt -
which all your words of beauty ever spelt -
not comrade, no, nor consort, understood
how much that pain had wracked your seeking soul,
not knowing if your words would reach the world.
Dear Pilgrim of an ancient Brotherhood,
still you leap skyward to your glorious goal.

And you still love, Beloved,
with that same love you ever felt,
each vision that your great words ever spelt.
Oh heart of every heart!
Cor Cordium!

2004-03-05
Dedicated to Shelley, and all his present day followers

6 -   Loyauté Me Lie

Loyalty Binds me to my God,
Now and when I'm under sod.

Loyalty binds me to my wife
Who is more precious than my life.

Loyalty binds me to our love -
A very blessing from Above.

Loyalty binds me to our son,
He whose life is just begun.

Loyalty binds me to my friends,
With whom I share all goodly ends.

Loyalty binds me to this Land,
Which I defend with heart and hand.

Loyalty binds me to my crown,
Which I'll not cravenly lay down.
And still, Loyalty binds me.

A play on the motto of King Richard III.. March 2015.

7 -   The Arboretum

Too beautiful to describe
they stretch along the ride,
far too sweet for words
the song of birds;
some shy blooms
of cyclamen,
a few late roses.
And the air is clean
sweet and fresh,
as never in a town.
A blessing on the man
who this began!
May his monument
be these great
Redwood trees,
oaks and tall pine.
May they never fall,
but still stand, tall
against the skyline,
over grasses mown -
but gently; dug by moles
around the lime tree boles.
Stillness; a mild breeze
that whispers through these trees -
green Nature, and sweet Peace.

September 2014 Westonbirt

8 - Wiltshire Vale

Hills rise around, green, and gentle
dotted with chalk, and orchid-gemmed,
making a shallow vale where winds
the narrow river, snaking by;
and there above, man-made, the hill
called Silbury; of age unknown,
its purpose all un-guessed at still.
In the Hill's side a fold, a place
where a new birth could once be made:
an ancient, holy, folded space
used long ago for gaining grace:
on its top corpses were laid out
to be reduced by Nature, air:
the bones were gathered then, with care,
to be where the forefathers were:
nearby, surrounded by white stones,
the barrow where were placed those bones.
What wonders once were made here!
Stone on stone, chamber and passage,
the corbelled roof precisely made
to hold the relics of the tribe –
the bones of the forebears, buried here –
while over-head there flew a hawk –
today a merlin strikes its prey,
toward the wood she flies away,
taking her catch to waiting brood -
What changes, then, through centuries?
Flowers, bright grass, white stones, blue skies,
seen by us, and by those ancient men
living in this green land: we now, they then.

2004-08-27

9 - Snowdon

A sudden flush of heather on the mountainside,
the white smoke curling from a cottage fire;
Snowdon emerges, glorious, from the mist
Yr Wydda!Land of heights and air!
Some tumbled walls; a careful, tended Church
by strict circumference of a chestnut tree,
breathless, in green of newly opened leaves:
a place enclosed in verdure.
Fields traced by small streams, and by stone walls;
elms stand, fanned against the sky –
extremes of beauty where the hills meet high,
and mountains melt in mist.
Then sudden beauty of the springing corn,
cross-hatched by tourists,
seeded by sheep and the un-herded lambs;
may in its glory, hawthorn in its gay,
hailing the sun with bright, uplifted arms.
The mountains, rising smooth as light;
foreground furze-filled, wind etched, carved by rain;
white and black, beyond the blue,
their violet distance shines, fretted and patched
by falls of rock, gold-glimmering glints, in grass.
Black, and frowning at the azure sky,
great pylons stride like giants on the hills -
those interwoven hills laced with small streams -
the Kestrel swims across a sea of cloud,
dips, like a "kingfisher catching fire",*
into the blue beyond of mountain air,
Yr Wyddfa – loud with birds,
replete with beauty!

1999 *G.M Hopkins.

10 - Ripples

I will cast a stone
into a pond;
the ripples will spread.

I will cast a prayer
into the world,
let it be led
to the farthest shore.

I will cast my heart
into the air,
my loving heart will shed
my loving care
into the void
to reach the loveless.

Let my heart be set
where love is not,
and where no prayers
are said.

1999.

11 - For Sam

You are newly born,
do you remember before
when, safe inside
you heard your mother's heart
beat gently to a tune
that only you could hear?

You are just begun,
are you still wise,
with those wide eyes
that look upon the world,
no trace of fear?

You have just arrived,
do you recall the song
your mother sang, as she travelled,
carrying you along?

Do you know you are beautiful,
dear Child who's just arrived,
Great-grand-son, newly born,
come to be loved
by all who love you, Sam!
Remember that we love you!

12 - British Dragon

See how She writhes!
From Avebury
to Glastonbury
her long loops, lithe,
circle and encircle
circled stones.
She-dragon of the land,
star-crowned She lies
along the hills
where earth meets skies,
there She writhes!
She is the Goddess,
Divine Feminine,
Lady of this realm
from ancient days:
her un-sleeping dream
to keep her children hale;
nurturing the rills
that run along the vales
where She drinks dew,
and, drinking, thrives.
This British Dragon
blossom-scaled with love,
blessing all She looks on –
stand now at Silbury,
when all around
is moated-in with rain,
and see again
how this lithe Lady writhes!
2003

13 - Welcome Home

(For KR, Poet. d. July 2003)

So you have been swallowed
by that bright water-ring
you so much loved
and suffered for.

Gone beyond bodies now,
spirits can blend
in fearless, lust-less, laughter;
your voice can sing
in unison with Nature,
and with him whose love
was not the love of women,
but who loved your soul.

You can rise to where the trees
breathe out their cleansing air,
where all your loves and pains are one,
and all are pacified and gone:
no need now for the blame you laid
upon yourself;

Your lifted soul will judge life –
all its woes, and trials, and tragedies -
joyously rising through the songs you made
to join with who you truly loved,
and truly made
the centre of your life,
outside your Poet's fate.
Arising, you will find it's never late
when you have given so much love –
such charity!
 2003

14 - Valle Crucis Abby

This hill of golden leaves enfolds and guards
a sacred ruin, built of honeyed stone,
reflected in blue water. Was it here
that, long ago ,one wise man visioned clear
the great Welsh Law?
Can you imagine him as he bestrode
this quiet valley, reached by quiet road,
tracing the brackened slope beneath the trees,
his leather sandals laced below his knees,
cloaked in his mantle made of native wool,
his silver brooch set with chalcedony?
And as he strode these hills, untiring, he
Turned, in his wise mind's eye, that careful Code
That told his countrymen how they might be
true to each other, to themselves, to God.
So is not this still sacred earth?
For here his ancient Codex had its birth,
long before England's worn and patchwork quilt
of Saxon and of Norman laws was built.
For this man, Father to his countrymen,
brooded on what was serviceable then,
and brought it forth, if not between these walls -
this abbey with its arcades and its halls -
then in this place, and in this very scene
where water keeps the fair land fresh and green,
and summer lush with vegetation's grace,
and winter's frosts the twigs of ash trees trace.
He breathed the crisp air, heady as good wine,
and felt his spirit touched by the Divine;
on mountains where he knew each stone and rock,
and tree that grew there; watched the fleecy flock.
Did he pick blueberries to slake his thirst,
and drink clear water from the springs that burst
unsparingly from mountainside and stone?

Escaping the Housework Book Three
While musing here to rest him, did he own
to his most inner vision, holy, wise,
the writ that ran in every wise man's eyes,
before this fair and lovely place was stolen
from its true owners, grasped and broken
by bloody spear, and strangers' foreign speech?
And are there now still men whose sight will reach
his words of wisdom, that were written then?
And did the nation's Father watch the sheep
like puffs of mist all littered on the deep
of these lush fields and this green slope
so free, and frisking in their Nation home?
Or did he notice, in the coming gloam
of evening's dimness, the star's clear reflection
shining in these bright waters of perfection
that mirror now the broken abbey walls,
still sweet with incense from the ancient days?
We, too, who visit now should stop and praise,
not just this lovely ruin, but the man
whose clear enlightenment and perfect plan
gave promise to his country men, of peace,
of simple justice, and of sweet release
from all barbarity –'til Norman hands
tore down the Dragon Banner, stole the lands!
Yet all is peaceful now, and glows with gold –
Nature recaptures what men's laws can't hold –
the wide blue water and the wooded hill,
Abaty Glyn Y Groes, lovely still
in gracious desolation. Recall, then,
Hwyl Dda, and what he gave his countrymen!

2000

15 - Treorchy Male Voice Choir.

Men singing –
not rolling from pubs
drunk and reeling,
but honing
voice, and skill, and feeling
to join together
in performing melodies
of power and beauty –
a ringing
paean of praise
filling the hall
with harmony,
pressed down and running over
into hearts that hear,
into the waiting ear;
old songs from Wales,
all sung mellifluously
in Welsh – a tongue
well suited to the tune
of lovely song.

Ordinary men
making together
extraordinary art,
that heals the soul,
the spirit, and the heart;
that makes eyes weep
for beauty of the sound
of voices truly bound
by custom and by love
for what each sings -
Treorchy's kings!

2/6/2001

16 - These Stones

They rise from a fine mist of seeding grass:
sudden and rugged, grey and stoical,
old as the Sphynx, and as inscrutable,
creating this enclosed and sacred space
with wind that makes no sound, a silent gale,
blowing the smoke and scene of ancient myths
across these deep, steep, turf-clad earthen walls.
These stones here are a magnet in their force,
drawing the skin, the flesh, the very bone
and marrow of their chosen people home.
Massive and stalwart, yet not threatening,
they make the refuge of the Island Race:
a place of silence and of sanctity,
but of no awesome dread - just mystery.
Touched by the sun, rain-veiled, or swathed in mist
whatever weather, they are beautiful –
the coming-home is perfect, full of peace.
Whatever ritual was here performed,
ages have washed away the slightest taint
of blood or anguish, or of terror now.
These tall Stones like delivered mothers lie,
cleansed, drained, and warmed by birth and history;
only to touch them is to feel the Earth
moving in rhythm with the Stellar pull;
to walk within is to experience
that silent storm that lifts men from their feet,
and raises up the soul to read the myths
made by past ages to explain away
Avebury's most exact polarity.
This ancient ring of stones that stand within
their mighty bulwarks, dug by mighty men,
and blessed by Holy Women, long ago,
as Shrine and Centre for a holy Vow,
still potent in these brooding, breeding stones,

breathing their ancient magic on the air.
The soundless draught of power in the Rings;
catches imagination, spirit, too;
bathing in mystery-believing fire,
the mind dwells deeply on these ancient rows -
forerunners of knot-garden and of maze;
where Green-Men wake, and Summer Queens are borne,
now placid, pregnant sheep graze peacefully,
and Ancient Britain lives on, perfectly.

2003

17 - The Siren's song to Odysseus

Sitting and singing where the shining waves
dash, ever angry, through the coral caves,
I hold my mirror and my golden comb,
singing sweet songs of my deep-sea home.
So sweetly I sing them, not to scare
Odysseus, bound to his ship's mast there!
He has stopped with wax every crew-man's ear
so that none of his rowers hear,
and blindfolded them, so they cannot see
my glittering hair, and swim to me.
O my wily Greek sailor, bound with strings!
you'll writhe with a passion that burns and stings
seeing you face in my looking glass,
your lust reflected, as your ship slides past!
For so it has been since time begun,
and so forever have Sirens sung,
with a golden comb and s a silver harp
to lure the sailors to corals sharp,
where tempting billows hide angry caves
that hunger beneath the swelling waves:
I'll caress you, possess you, and swim you through
as every Siren was born to do –
but, wily Greek sailor, I waste my breath
for my song does not lure you to your death,
no matter how sweetly the words are sung
of the age of Time since the World begun!
Wise Odysseus! You twist in your bonds
as you see the beautiful sea-green fronds
of my glorious, rippling, strangling hair,
as you stand, still bound, at your ship's mast there.
Your sailors have bound you, but not so tight –
come break your bonds for they are but light!
Come, sit with me and discourse of love
as the sharp stars sparkle in night above:

Escaping the Housework Book Three
perhaps you pine for Penelope
as you strive with your ropes to struggle free –
Come! Love with me in my coral lair,
and learn to tame my green strangling hair –
but his boat glides past me like a bird,
and only the wise old Greek has heard
as I sing to my silver harp the rhyme
of the start of Life and the end of Time!
 2004

18 - The Pyrenees

Why do I want to be there?
Truly, it is the mountains –
they rise, dark against the sky,
so amazing, natural,
full of green grace, but rugged.
Then, in the upper pastures,
autumn crocus – fields of them -
there scented herbs and flowers
assault the sense with beauty:
and you understand why
folk make perfume here –
at the mountains foot
lavender blossoms
and clear spring water
make you long to invent
some wonderful new scent.
While, on the lower levels
the restaurant's food
is almost heavenly!
The mountains, and the people –
'Les Gens du Sud' -
warm, friendly, a delight:
that's why I want to be there –
that's just why!

August 27th 2014

19 - The Fair Venetian

In silk and velvet see my lady go,
into her gondola, to meet
her latest noble inamorato!
Watch how her dainty feet
perch on the cushions of the boat.
The gondolier, with careful craft,
steers windward, so her golden ringlets float
around her shoulders in the draught;
brocades as rich as forest leaves
she wears, her breathless bosom bare,
with gold and silver, pearl-strewn sleeves.
Music accompanies her journey there,
as down the Grand Canal she glides,
where the jeunesse doree of Venice rides.
Now at a kiosk, built for lust, she lands,
helped from the boat by one who finds
her skin so soft beneath his eager hands!
And so she glides, this fair Venetian girl!
They say that Venice is the pearl
of cities – true it is, this lovely whore
is fair as any gem the Doges wore!

Suggested by the film, "The honest Courtesan"
1999

20 - Poljigga

I saw two grey seals greeting
in a Cornish bay; their meeting
was elegant and loving
as, through the water moving
like mermaids, they embraced.
Years of forgetfulness had chased
that picture from my mind
I have been so blind!
They met and loved, without a ring
to sanctify their partnering:
and so perhaps should we embrace
love, when it comes, with joyful face,
as naturally as those two did -
and yet I have forever hid
my love from those I care for -
usually not dared for -
I should have learned from the wild:
it's too late now for me- a foolish child,
I made my lover flee:
I sent him far away.

21 - Old Age

So this is peace!
Youth's fires are now a gentle glow,
one does not strive for mere appearances,
one had much better stay than go,
contentment this!
The world can pass us by
without ambition tearing at the heart,
the centre is no longer, "Me" and "My",
but resignation!
For things not done will not be, now:
no matter, for the time is sweet,
and light is kinder when the logs burn low!

22 - Mendelson's Hebridean Suite

'How lovely the sea is'
the music sings:
water washes in:
the cavern echoes,
black basalt rising round
unchangeable
sends water crashing,
against rocks,
make sounds increase;
the cunning sea,
tricking the eye, the ear,
both to see and hear
how lovely the sea is!
How deep the water!
Now the gushing wave
of elegant music,
played on singing strings,
is sonic as the rocks
that echo sounds
at Fingal's cave!

July 2014

23 - 'Look in my pockets, Duckie'

My Grandfather,
in his silk and cashmere suit,
made me fish through
all his many pockets.
In the innermost,
waist-coat, hidden one
were sweets or dried fruit,
perhaps a sixpence!
They were for Spring, -
'The voice of the turtle
is heard in the land.'
(I did not know the turtle
was a dove!)
and pressed into my hand
with Grandpa's love.
Now we could eat
our winter stores,
'For new growth cometh'.
In Autumn,
when all my friends
looked to Halloween,
we celebrated New Year –
not Autumn, or closure,
but an opening,
not withstanding
Winter's chill,
this was a beginning –
through dead leaves rustling
around our feet,
we found arising
shoots of Spring,
a new promise –
and life was sweet!   29/09/2014

24 - Gloriana

I am the Lion's cub. I go robed in silk,
my bodkin-slender fingers white as milk.
The virgin of the unicorn am I,
my father's daughter, with his golden eye.
And I will work for England 'til my end,
whatever God, or Pope, or Spaniard send!
And I will dance, so that my people see
none is so active, nor so brave, as me.
In this my land there's none who loves me not,
yet there is none for whom I'd give one jot
of my ascendancy, virginity!
For they were all that stood twixt death and me
when Mary lit her fires for heresy.
Burnings! I will do justice when I can,
I peer not into consciences of man,
nor look into mens' hearts – I need not so,
for every true man's heart is mine, I know!
I am Elizabeth, England's glory -
I know my people tell my story,
nor wait for me to die before they say
"Elizabeth is great, and good her sway!"
And so I wear my royal father's crown,
dressed like an icon in my golden gown;
and I must hide my wrinkles with white paste,
to be their fair Diana, youthful, chaste.
I 'm such a legend never seen before –
child of great Harry, and of Ann – his whore!

2000

25 - Friendship and love

There is a kind of Love that silent stays,
that yearns on the beloved, sighs, and prays
only for what is good and right
to be around the loved ones, in their sight.
So is my love for all my dearest friends
who gather round in friendship – not for ends
of their own wishing: so my open heart
allows them, when they will, to enter or depart.
and it is this that brings the Healing Bliss
of Love, for everything that lives, and is.
Are you troubled? Then my love will soothe
your heart, and make your pathway smooth.
Are you grieving? Then comforting Love
will fly from me to you, as birds above
fly quickly to their hungry, crying young
to feed them, and then sing their sweetest song.
Are you lonely? Then my love will gently bring
another soul to company your sad soul's spring.
This is not love as by the world beheld,
debased and cheapened, spirit all withheld;
but clean and fresh, and pure affection, mine,
that will not see the souls I love repine.
Come, rest upon the solace I extend -
in friendship's name my heart I lend
to comfort, solace and accompany -
whatever you might wish for, that will I be.
No hardened marble dwells within my breast,
for I can laugh or sorrow, with the rest:
can bring you joy and simple fun
in dreary torrent or in warming sun –
true Friendship lives to serve, and serves to live,
and ever pure and simple Love will give.

© SAC March 2005

26 - Married Love

It is when, simultaneously, we
fall into inconsequential laughter:
or when suddenly, unanimously,
we burst into singing the same old song,
as we walk the long white Downs along,
under the golden cheerfulness of sun:
when we reach tenderly, hand seeking hand,
as we stroll onward on the shining sand,
while the white seagulls wheel and call above –
it's then we recognise our state of Love.
When, as a duo, we both take up arms
fighting a malady, or such alarms,
working and caring for each others' good,
that we know we both love as lovers should.
Come then, together we will laugh and sing,
and love, and walk together into Spring!

27 - Egypt, Dying

Silent, sinuous, serpentine,
with cat's sleep-laden, sexy eyes;
bejewelled: dressed in finest stuff,
pleated, and edged with silken thread,
her great crown golden on her head,
pacing the temple, over marble floor
diaphanous she drifts;
between the columns,
between day and night.

Upon her brow the Serpent of Two Lands;
a woven basket held between her hands
filled full of figs – and more.
She who held Egypt in her sway,
and Caesar in her arms,
most beautiful and charming, mighty She;
a Grecian queen with Egypt's mystery,
too proud, too beautiful, too brave,
to grace Augustus' triumph as a slave.
Majestic, soft and silent – see,
Cleopatra comes.

Between the city and the sands,
making most royal sacrifice, she stands,
arms raised in plea or blessing,
offering now her holiest gifts,
calling on Isis and the Gods,
protective Spirits upon whom she leans.
Too dignified to turn and flee -
from the rush basket in her hands,
between day and the night,
between dark and the Light,
between the city and the sands -
A snake will make her free.

28 - Displaced Person

Rachel has shed less tears than I;
I am the tortured wind and rain,
I the epitome of pain,
the hounded clouds across the sky.

Job knew less bitterness than I!
I am of sufferers the chief –
I the embodiment of grief,
the out-cast and the homeless, I.

Ruth was less desolate than I;
the hopeless stranger in the storm,
I, ever exiled from my home,
the eternal nomad, I.

No homely place to dwell have I.
I am the dust across the plain –
not to be gathered up again,
of a scattered nation, I!

29 - Crossing

They were crossing,
a long, long line of them,
men, women, children,
each carrying a burden,
trying not to hurry,
trying not to worry.
Concerned about possible
pursuit and slaughter,
onward they headed,
walking a dry path –
which was a wonder-
until, like thunder,
the sound of horses -
the pursuit they'd dreaded!
Hastily they threaded
their way to the other shore,
then they heard the roar
of waters dashing,
meeting and crashing -
men and horses, losing
life, as they drowned,
as the sea closed around.
A woman began to sing aloud,
a song of joy,
but from a cloud
a great voice spoke
the echoes woke
like someone frowning
'How dare you sing,
when my children are drowning!"
The Hebrew girl was silenced.

September 2104

30 - At Crickley Hill

As I walked over Crickley Hill
a woman walked beside;
her woollen gown much like my own.
her brogued foot matched my stride.
Her coat of bear-skin, fur-side out,
was better than my nylon clout!
"Well, sister, now how much has changed?"
she asked me, as we strode:
"Food in the pot, the children well,
warm, safe, in our abode.
The man I chose be strong and fit –
and would you not agree -
two thousand years between us ranged,
yet you're the same as me!"

As I walked over Crickley Hill,
a woman fell in step,
her garments were much like my own,
she carried a rush skep.
And as we walked beneath the sky
we could have been as one
although two thousand years had passed
since her short day was done.
"It's only Love," she said to me,
"that makes the whole world turn, you see.
A happy man, and food, and health
for children, is the only wealth"
She spoke the truth, the Iron Age lass
who strode beside me through the grass.
And I knew well she spoke no ill,
the ghost who walked on Crickley Hill.

At Crickley 1995

31 - The Cladagh Ring

Two hands that hold a heart
a sign of love and trust:
the ring my love wore;
which he gave to me:
I wished no diamond,
just the sign I saw
when I was three,
or thereabouts,
carved on a stone –
'Crusader's Heart Tomb,
a heart his friend brought home'
explained the sign.
So, when I saw that ring,
I knew the man was mine –
for there it was:
of love and trust the sign -
that he could and would
hold my heart fast
he did - and still he does,

September 2014

32 - Au Revoir

Watch for me in starlight,
that is when I'll come,
stealing gently through the night,
a small flame in the gloam.

Watch for me in Springtime,
that's when I'll be near,
when leaves flourish round the lime
and the blue sky's clear.

Watch for me in Summer,
 when the rose's scent
whispers round the garden bower
where I so often leant.

Look for me in Autumn,
when the apples fall
underneath the yellow leaves,
and robins change their call.

Look for me in Winter,
when the wind is cold,
round about the fireplace
where the warm flame's gold.

Look for me in starlight,
 I'll be always there,
to share your pleasure and delight
in the evening air.
 2004

33 - When You and I Were Young

When you and I were young, Lad,
and both still in our teens,
and you were bold as princes,
and I was proud as queens,
you gave your heart to me, Lad,
and I gave mine to you,
for all the world was full of dreams,
and all the dreams were new.
But on the pages of our hearts
we both wrote different names,
and both of us have rowed our boats
on very different streams.
Yet, deep inside my heart, Lad,
there's still a place for you
that nobody can take away,
though I'm a wife, and true.
And sometimes in my glass, Lad,
I see the wrinkles there,
and wonder where I went Lad,
and further, where did you?
So very deep within, Lad,
and hidden from all view,
I 'm still your little queen, Lad,
and you're my brave prince, too!

1999

34 - Valentine

Now it is the start offspring
when the sweet birds start to sing
and blossoms form on trees above
while thoughts turn to the god of Love.

So to Eros will I turn,
hoping his goodwill to earn
offering to him this heart -
though from yours I cannot part.

To each other we're bespoken,
so this chain cannot be broken
that stretches out when we're apart,
and joins my heart, still, to your heart!

1999.February. for Fun.

35 - Bob Dylan

Don't listen to Dylan
if you are sick.
Don't listen to him if
your bones won't stick
together one more day –
he'll break your heart
with what he'll say
before you part,
before your body's stiff!

Don't listen to his song
if you can't stand
the dark of night –
don't understand
it'll be alright
when dawn comes on,
when you feel strong,
you're in the light!

Listen to Dylan
when you can be wise,
when you can see the sun,
and are ready to rise
and not be dark
or changeful,
when you don't want
to be "half done".
Enjoy his verse
before he's gone,
when you want
to know the worst
about Life's song!

Don't listen to Dylan

Escaping the Housework Book Three
if you can't kick
habits of convention,
throw a brick
for freedom through the pane
glazing contention
with sweet lying words;

Listen to Dylan
when you are strong
to stand alone,
to string along
the politician
and the drone –
hear Bob Dylan's song!

36 - When Dylan Dropped in.

I am talking, kind friend,
about my ancestors,
that line without an end
of Welsh Joneses – mine,
and maybe yours as well.
I'll write as you require
of Wales: water, hills, vales,
the shore-line; I aspire
to record Welsh beauty –
I hope for all posterity:
and that you will enjoy
what I wrote of Joneses:
all of them, lovely girls,
and every lovely boy,
with whom we share blood, bones:
our heritage is there:
I loved mountains, the sea :
thanks for letting me drop in to see
that we remember them,
now that we've reached this age:
 for they're both yours and mine,
our great Welsh Joneses heritage!

March 2015

37 - Bedtime

Rising to my window
comes the scent
of wet leaves and wisteria;
the first stars shimmer,
and a last thrush trills,
dusk moves across the hills.
After my day's work
soft white pillows
invite and cradle me,
but no sleep comes.
No Matter! Beauty breathes
around me – scent
and sound and sight
are all a great delight;
Peace settles like a duvet –
lulls all the long day's stress –
no sleep is needed!

2013

38 - Comming out of a Tunnel

Like coming from a tunnel
I begin to re-emerge,
not all of me of course,
but enough to feel the surge
of Life running its course –
enough to make it real,
to trust in what I feel,
after so long in the black,
I blink on coming back.
Scarred and battered though I be
unsure of health, I still can see,
where once I hoped for death,
a chance for life and light and breath,
and as an antidote to pain,
I start to think of life again,
halting, and timid of the end,
shyly, as greeting a new friend,
gingerly I look around,
for me the freedom is new ground!
This much I know: returning strength
begets the will to try the length,
the breadth of what is left me still
of Life – and live I will!
Slowly, as moths emerge
drying their wings, testing the urge
to fly, body and soul in me combine
to retake what was ever mine
of life and joy, whatever I could do,
I'll strive to do again, better and new!
The old me, returning, torn,
meets the new me, being born!

1998

39 - After Counselling

As from a tunnel I emerge
dazzled, from dark to light,
feeling suddenly a surge
of life – amazed delight,
as when a moth which dries its wings
tastes unfamiliar air -
at this release from care.
Death was once my only friend,
the cure for all my pain,
now I can see a different end
I'm free – I live again.
A lovely world surrounds me –
though I knew that it was there
I could not, for my sorrow see
that beauty was so near,
and darkness was in me.
I'd built myself a dungeon,
a dark, glass, prison cell
where I could live, be all alone,
could neither touch nor tell –
then there came one to listen,
truly hear what I'd to say,
who made the cold glass glisten,
'til it faded clean away.
Life may be long, it may be short –
I no longer care – the scope
of beauty, I've been taught,
lies within my eager reach-
perhaps my moth is labelled "Hope".

1997

40 - Pigeon

How beautiful these bones,
fragile and flexible,
and exactly jointed;
feathers perfect for flight.
Jumbled they lie,
still interesting.
The hawk has had its day,
fed from this bird, its prey,
leaving these lovely bones
laid upon my lawn.
The remains of a life
that was always wind-borne,
and ended tragically -
at least for this bird,
and its mate, alone,
sitting forlorn.
I feed the widowed bird,
hoping it may re-wed,
produce more of these
so beautiful bones
and perfect dove grey plumes.

March. 2015

41 - Ressuscitation

They snatched me from the boat,
a drowning child,
bringing me back to live
in this dark place.
No doubt they did the best,
they thought, for me.
But I would rather be
far out to sea
whence I could not return
again to strive.
Death's not the end of Life –
there is no end:
the cycle goes on round:
there are no dead.
Far out, beyond the sound
I'd rather be,
than here and half alive,
when all is said.
Had I but reached the island
what would I see?
A place so beautiful,
so full of peace,
in Love so plentiful,
where I could cease
to go on suffering –
but rescue came.
The drowning child lives
abiding time.......
2014

42 - Between the Adverts

In the intervals of silence,
while they try to sell us things,
I hear my brain thinking at last;
I can write, too, if I'm fast.
But mostly there is noise,
making me wish we'd use
less square entertainment,
and let me think; and, if I'm
lucky, write a few words:
may be a stanza, in the quiet.
That precious in-between
of silence!

May 2015

43 - The Red Kites land.

Its nest well hidden, the red kite rises,
thermal-riding, over the green of Wales,
where sheep, like cotton wool,
are scattered in the fields.
Where water shines in the lake
whilst winds kiss waves awake
and skylarks still make tune.
Silence and beauty! Calm
enough to make men brave
to fight for this sweet country, save
these hills and mountains,
and all that heavenly balm
that is the air of Wales.

Dolgoch Falls, September.1995

44 - Phaelenopsis

Perhaps it is the intricacy
that makes them look so simple;
this tiny curl of petal,
the dash of colour on white
that's so much less than more,
so the blooms become
exquisite, so alive.
Trying to draw them seems
almost impossible;
the mind is too complicated
to quite understand
such simple intricacy.

April,2015

45 - A Man of Light

There is a man who walks
with light around his head.
He could make a dark place bright,
far more than golden robes
that others wear. In his plain white
he makes a place of faith
that cannot be snuffed out
although theis place was taken
from his brothers, long ago,
yet he still carries that long,
holy ,flame of Light, full bright.
Into the singing, bell-filled dark,
he brings an ancient, veritable, spark.

23 April 2015.

46 - Best and Brightest

Alighting on each bloom,
spread-winged, drinking beauty,
taking and giving the divine life
of truth and light and poetry,
weighted, yet weightless in the world,
encumbered by what must be done,
needing the ballast of less feeling but
companionship of soul,
deep seated in the heaviness of strength
bearing its beauty lightly
joyful in sunlit mirth ,achieved from suffering
you hover on the poetry of life.
May this be yours then:
"each single blade of grass"*
finding support of loveliness
in one strong, questing, heart;
companionship that does not slip away
to dark and silent tombs of misery,
but rises, laughter still, a
"radiant" sister of the day",*
to lift and carry light -and levity-
as well as solemn thought,
perceptive understanding of your need-
may this your blessing be!

  ** Shelley.   2003

47 - Shelly at Tan Yr Allt

Your song was like a bird
singing at dusk, in Spring,
challenging music heard
from the rock's echoing.

Rising from the valley floor
trees abound in green,
leaning toward the terrace door
where once you could be seen,
you lover of birds and song!

Guest of this haunted place,
your stay was not for long
your life was homeless wandering.
You, seeking for Love's perfect face,
your heart forever wrung.

A casket held that heart,
that burnt, but would not burn,
your quest was love, ever to smart,
to suffer and to burn.

O singer of a matchless song,
dreamer of matchless dream,
you knew how the world should yearn
the poet's art to learn!

Your flight was like an eagle's climb
into the endless blue-
two hundred years is little time
for us to honour you!

Singer of the matchless song,
dreamer of matchless dreams!

Escaping the Housework Book Three
this one moment is too long-
two centuries an instant seems –
for we may miss a word, a phrase,
and be the poorer for the miss
and labour on, for all our days
lacking that most perfect bliss
with which you wrote your dream!
                              2000.

48 - Ancient Love

It was the scent of trodden grass
damp under naked foot;
white of wings as barn owls pass
seeking their night-time food.
It was the sight of willow trees
that followed winding stream
along the lush green water-leas
that filled my waking dreams.
No lover, now, lives in my heart
to take up al l my thought,
and I have lost htat happy art
of joy, that once I caught.
So creeps on now the grey of age
lost is the spring of youth,
but, written on my heart's last page
Is still the gold of Truth.
No more the crumpled sheet, the bed
warm with the scent of love;
at night time I lay down my head
chaste as cold Moon above.
But I remember still the days
when life was full of joy –
love, passing in a golden haze
for happy girl and boy;
and places where the grass was crushed
by lovers' winding arms
while, overhead, the flowers blushed
to see such sweet alarms!
So, sing a song of yester-year
and lays of yesterday,
when all around the valleys rang
with happiness, and lovers sang!
2012